MIND YOUR MANNERS
MASTERING ETIQUETTE IN THE WORKPLACE

OMRAN KHAYAMI

Copyright © 2024. All rights reserved.
No part of this book may be reproduced, distributed, or transmitted in any form or by any means, including photocopying, recording, or other electronic or mechanical methods, without the prior written permission of the author, except for brief excerpts in critical reviews or analyses.

Table of Contents

Preface: 5
Introduction: 7
Chapter 1: First Impressions Count 13
Chapter 2: Communication is Key 21
Chapter 3: Meeting Manners 31
Chapter 4: The Social Side of Work 41
Chapter 5: The Digital Workplace 49
Chapter 6: The Multicultural Workplace 57
Chapter 7: Everyday Etiquette 65
Chapter 8: Leadership and Etiquette 73
Chapter 9: Evolving Etiquette 81
Conclusion: Elevating Your Career Through the Power of Etiquette ... 89

Preface:

In the fast-evolving tapestry of workplace dynamics, etiquette often becomes the silent force steering the ship. While technical expertise and ambition might land you the job, it is the art of professional behavior that helps you thrive and grow in your career. This book is born from the realization that navigating the workplace requires more than just knowing your role; it demands an awareness of how your actions impact others and how to cultivate meaningful relationships.

Throughout my career, I've observed a recurring pattern: those who succeed aren't always the loudest voices or the most visible figures. Instead, they are the individuals who combine competence with consideration, blending skill with sincerity. Whether it's a firm handshake, a timely email reply, or the ability to manage cultural nuances in an increasingly global workplace, the small gestures often leave the most lasting impressions.

This book is both a guide and a companion—a resource to help you refine your approach to professional interactions. It doesn't preach rigid rules or archaic traditions; instead, it celebrates adaptability, empathy, and respect as the cornerstones of modern workplace etiquette. From mastering first impressions to tackling the challenges of remote work, each chapter offers practical advice, real-world examples, and actionable tips that you can immediately apply.

As you embark on this journey, I invite you to reflect on your current habits and interactions. What kind of professional legacy do you want to leave behind? How can you create an environment where kindness, respect, and professionalism thrive? These are the questions that inspired this book, and I hope they spark the same inspiration in you.

INTRODUCTION

Introduction:

Welcome to **Mind Your Manners: Mastering Etiquette in the Workplace**! Think of this book as your trusted companion, here to help you decode the often unspoken rules of professional behavior. In a world that's becoming increasingly interconnected, where cultural norms, communication styles, and even dress codes vary widely, understanding and mastering workplace etiquette is more critical—and rewarding—than ever. But don't worry; this isn't about stuffy traditions or rigid rules. It's about learning to navigate the professional world with confidence, ease, and grace.

Why does workplace etiquette matter? Imagine this scenario: You're at a critical client meeting, and one of your colleagues keeps interrupting the discussion, fiddling with their phone, and visibly disengaging. Now contrast that with another colleague who listens intently, contributes thoughtfully, and ends with a firm handshake and genuine smile. Who do you think left a better impression? That's the power of etiquette. It's not just about knowing what fork to use at a dinner meeting—it's about showing respect, building trust, and creating a lasting, positive impression in every interaction.

But here's the thing: good manners in the workplace are not just for "others." They benefit *you* as much as they benefit those around you. When you consistently display professionalism, you'll find that people are more likely to listen to your ideas, value your contributions, and support your career growth. Etiquette is like the oil in the engine of your career—it keeps things running smoothly, avoiding unnecessary friction and ensuring long-term success.

This book is packed with real-life examples, practical advice, and actionable tips to help you handle almost any situation with grace. Wondering how to introduce yourself to a high-ranking executive without fumbling over your words? Not sure how to politely end a conversation at an office party without seeming rude? What about navigating those tricky moments in a virtual meeting when everyone's talking over each other? We'll cover all that and more. From the basics of dressing appropriately for your workplace to the subtleties of cultural sensitivity in a global business environment, we'll arm you with the knowledge and confidence to shine in any professional setting.

Let's pause for a moment to reflect on some relatable scenarios. Have you ever accidentally sent an email without proofreading it, only to realize later that it contained an embarrassing typo? Maybe you've witnessed a colleague arriving late to a meeting, unprepared and frazzled, setting a tone of disorganization for the entire discussion. Or perhaps you've seen the opposite—a coworker who always remembers birthdays, greets everyone with a warm "good morning," and knows how to gently but firmly resolve conflicts.

These small moments can have a significant impact on how others perceive you and your ability to lead, collaborate, and succeed in the workplace.

Etiquette also plays a key role in building relationships. Think about the times someone made you feel truly seen and respected—a thoughtful thank-you note, a sincere compliment on a job well done, or even the simple act of remembering your name after one meeting. These gestures may seem small, but they have a ripple effect, creating goodwill and fostering trust. Now imagine becoming the kind of professional who naturally inspires that level of respect and connection. That's what this book aims to help you achieve.

As workplaces evolve, so do the rules of engagement. Remote work, for instance, has added new layers of complexity. How do you create a strong virtual presence when you're just a thumbnail on someone's screen? Should you always have your camera on during meetings? And what about managing time zones when working with international teams? In today's fast-paced, tech-driven world, digital etiquette is just as important as knowing how to behave in an office setting. We'll explore all these modern challenges and provide you with clear, actionable strategies to handle them like a pro.

Here's another truth: good etiquette is contagious. When you lead with kindness, respect, and professionalism, you set the tone for those around you. Your team becomes more cohesive, your workplace more pleasant, and your career trajectory brighter. You don't need to be perfect—everyone makes mistakes—but by committing to small, intentional improvements, you can make a big impact.

And let's not forget the joy that comes with mastering etiquette. When you know how to navigate tricky situations—whether it's responding to a passive-aggressive email or gracefully excusing yourself from a tedious conversation—you'll feel a sense of empowerment and control. Instead of dreading interactions, you'll approach them with confidence, knowing that you have the tools to handle anything that comes your way.

This book isn't just about learning to be polite; it's about unlocking your potential to connect, lead, and thrive in the workplace. You'll learn how to adapt to different environments, bridge cultural gaps, and even turn awkward moments into opportunities. By the end of this journey, you'll be equipped not only to succeed professionally but also to enjoy the process.

So, let's embark on this journey together. Whether you're just starting out in your career, stepping into a leadership role, or navigating the complexities of a multicultural team, there's something here for you. Together, we'll explore the art and science of workplace etiquette, transforming the way you work, connect, and grow. Let's make every workday smoother, every interaction more meaningful, and every opportunity a chance to shine. Shall we get started?

1 FIRST IMPRESSIONS COUNT

Chapter 1: First Impressions Count

The Unforgettable First Encounter

Think back to a time when you met someone new at work. Maybe it was your boss, a client, or a colleague. Without realizing it, you made a mental checklist—what they wore, how they spoke, even the energy they brought into the room. You probably made your judgment in under 30 seconds. That's the power of first impressions.

For instance, when Ahmed joined his first job at a consulting firm, he arrived in a wrinkled shirt and scuffed shoes, thinking it wouldn't matter since he was "just a trainee." What he didn't realize was that his team was judging his attention to detail from the moment he walked in. It took months of overcompensating through stellar work to overcome that initial perception.

First impressions are like sticky notes. Once someone attaches an idea to you, it's hard to peel off. Fortunately, you can take charge of how people perceive you right from the start. The keys? Your appearance, behavior, and communication style.

Dressing for Success: Clothes Speak Louder Than Words

Your outfit is often the first thing people notice, even before you say "hello." Dressing appropriately signals respect for the workplace, your colleagues, and yourself. It doesn't have to mean designer labels or a three-piece suit. What matters is that your attire aligns with your professional environment.

Understanding Your Workplace's Dress Code

Every workplace has an unwritten rulebook when it comes to clothing. Some environments lean toward ultra-formal business attire, while others embrace Silicon Valley's hoodie culture. The trick is understanding what's expected without losing your personal style.

- **Example:** On her first day at a tech company, Fatima wore a tailored suit, thinking it would help her stand out. She did—but not in the way she hoped. The team joked about her "boardroom chic" look in their casual, jeans-and-sneakers office. While Fatima quickly adjusted, she learned the hard way to research workplace norms beforehand.

Here are some tips to decode your workplace dress code:

- **Observe Colleagues:** Look at how leaders dress. If your boss wears a blazer over jeans, that's your clue.
- **Ask HR:** If you're unsure, a quick email to HR can clarify expectations.
- **Play it Safe:** When in doubt, lean toward formal for the first few days. It's easier to dress down later than to recover from looking underdressed.

Navigating Different Dress Codes

Here's a quick guide to dressing for various workplace environments:

1. **Formal Business Attire:** Think law firms, banks, and corporate offices.
    - **Men:** A tailored suit in neutral tones, polished shoes, and a conservative tie.
    - **Women:** A pantsuit or skirt suit, closed-toe shoes, and minimal jewelry.
2. **Business Casual:** Found in creative industries, startups, and some corporate offices.
    - **Men:** Pants or jeans, a button-down shirt, and optional blazer.

- **Women:** A blouse with a skirt or trousers, paired with flats or low heels.
3. **Casual:** Popular in tech and creative sectors.
    - Neat jeans, clean sneakers, and a polished shirt or sweater can work. Avoid sloppy, torn, or overly loud attire.
4. **Hybrid Workwear:** For remote workers, "Zoom-ready" attire has become a thing.
    - Keep your top half professional with a blazer or blouse. Sweatpants? Acceptable only if they're off-camera.

The Psychology of Introductions: Making Your Hello Count

You've dressed the part. Now comes the next hurdle: your introduction. Whether it's saying hello to a new team or meeting a client, how you present yourself in those first moments can set the tone for your relationship.

The Perfect Handshake

The handshake is a timeless symbol of confidence and respect. But did you know there's a science to it?

- **Tips for the Ideal Handshake:**
    - **Firmness:** Strike a balance. Too limp feels disengaged; too firm comes off as aggressive.
    - **Timing:** Hold for about 2-3 seconds.
    - **Eye Contact:** Look the other person in the eye while smiling to show warmth.
    - **Example:** During a client pitch, Ali's overly enthusiastic handshake almost crushed the client's fingers. He quickly adjusted, and his future handshakes became firm but friendly.

Introducing Yourself with Confidence

The way you introduce yourself leaves an impression long after the handshake ends.

- **Be Clear:** "Hi, I'm Zainab, the new project coordinator." Clear and simple.
- **Show Interest:** Add a follow-up, like "It's great to meet someone with so much experience in [field]."
- **Pro Tip:** Repeating the other person's name can help you remember it. "Nice to meet you, Ahmed. Ahmed, what's your role here?"

Addressing Titles and Formalities

Titles matter, especially in workplaces with strict hierarchies or cultural nuances. When in doubt, use formal titles like "Dr.," "Mr.," or "Ms." until invited to do otherwise.

- **Scenario:** During her internship in Japan, Layla quickly learned to address everyone with honorifics like "San" or "Sama." It impressed her colleagues and helped her build trust.

The Hidden Power of Body Language

First impressions aren't just about what you wear or say; they're also about how you carry yourself. Your body language can either reinforce or undermine your verbal communication.

- **Stand Tall:** Good posture conveys confidence.
- **Smile:** A genuine smile can make you more approachable and likable.
- **Avoid Crossed Arms:** It can signal defensiveness, even if you're just cold!

- **Real-Life Insight:** At a networking event, Sawsan noticed her friend Ebrahim seemed to repel people despite his polished pitch. Why? He kept glancing at his phone and standing with his arms crossed. After Ebrahim consciously worked on maintaining eye contact and open gestures, his networking success skyrocketed.

Business Card Etiquette: A Small Gesture with Big Impact

In a world dominated by LinkedIn and digital connections, business cards might feel outdated. But in many cultures, they remain a symbol of professionalism.

How to Exchange Cards

1. Offer your card with both hands in countries like Japan or China.
2. Receive cards with gratitude—read the details before putting it away.
3. Avoid scribbling notes on someone's card during the meeting.

- **Example:** During a conference in Dubai, Hasan accidentally crumpled a card he received, thinking it was unimportant. His action offended the giver, costing him a potential partnership.

Turning First Impressions into Lasting Impressions

First impressions are the beginning of the Example. To sustain that initial positive impact, consistency is key:

- **Be Reliable:** If you promised to send a follow-up email, do it promptly.
- **Engage with Enthusiasm:** Show interest in colleagues' ideas and efforts.

- **Maintain Appearance:** A polished look shouldn't fade after your first week.
- **Example:** Consider Reem, who impressed her team during her first week with punctuality and enthusiasm. But over time, her tardiness and lack of follow-through chipped away at their trust. The lesson? A great start needs consistent effort to maintain.

Action Plan for Nailing First Impressions

Here's your checklist for mastering first impressions:

1. **Prepare Your Look:** Keep a versatile wardrobe that aligns with your workplace culture.
2. **Practice Introductions:** Rehearse a confident, warm introduction with friends or mentors.
3. **Mind Your Body Language:** Stand tall, smile, and maintain eye contact.
4. **Carry Tools of the Trade:** Business cards, a professional notebook, or even a polished pen show you're ready.
5. **Follow Through:** Whether it's replying to emails or showing up on time, consistency cements your credibility.

Making a stellar first impression isn't about perfection—it's about preparation, awareness, and a touch of confidence. By investing in how you present yourself and interact with others, you're not just opening doors; you're ensuring they stay open. So, the next time you step into a room, remember: every detail counts. What impression will you leave today?

2 COMMUNICATION IS KEY

Chapter 2: Communication is Key

Communication is the lifeblood of every organization. It's how ideas are shared, collaborations are encouraged, and conflicts are resolved. Yet, it's one of the most common areas where things can go awry. Whether it's a poorly worded email, an awkward video call, or a tense conversation, missteps in communication can ripple through a workplace, causing misunderstandings, inefficiencies, and even resentment. This chapter dives deeply into the essentials of workplace communication, providing tips, examples, and actionable advice to ensure your interactions—whether written, spoken, or digital—are clear, respectful, and effective.

Email Etiquette: The Art of Writing Right

Emails are a cornerstone of modern work life. They're quick, convenient, and leave a written record, but they're also a breeding ground for miscommunication. A single misplaced word or an overly long message can derail a conversation or tarnish your professional image. Let's break down the components of effective email communication.

1. Mastering the Subject Line

Your subject line is your email's first impression, and like any first impression, it counts. It should be clear, concise, and relevant.

- **Examples of Great Subject Lines:**
    - For a meeting request: "Proposal Review Meeting – Thursday 3 PM"
    - For project updates: "Project Alpha: Status Update & Next Steps"
- **What to Avoid:**
    - "Hi" or "URGENT!!!" – These lack clarity and can either annoy or stress the recipient unnecessarily.

- **Pro Tip:** If your email is part of an ongoing thread, update the subject line if the content shifts. For instance, change "Initial Proposal" to "Updated Proposal with Feedback."

2. Greetings That Hit the Right Note

The tone of your greeting sets the stage for the entire email. Choose it based on the relationship and context.

- **Formal Contexts:** Use "Dear [Name]" or "Hello [Name]."
- **Casual Settings:** "Hi [Name]" or simply "[Name]," works well.
- **Avoid Over-Familiarity:** Using "Hey" or omitting a greeting altogether can feel abrupt or unprofessional.

Example: A colleague once accidentally addressed the CEO as "Buddy" due to an autocomplete error. The resulting awkward silence in the meeting could have been cut with a knife.

3. Structuring the Body of the Email

The body is where your message lives. Make it concise yet thorough.

- **Use Short Paragraphs:** Aim for 2-3 sentences per paragraph. Long blocks of text are daunting.
- **Bullet Points for Clarity:** For emails with multiple points, use bullet points to break up the content.
- **Action-Oriented Language:** Be clear about what you're asking. Instead of "Let me know your thoughts," write, "Please review the attached report and provide feedback by Friday."

4. Tone and Professionalism

Tone can make or break an email.

- **Keep it Professional:** Even when you're frustrated, resist the urge to let your emotions show.
- **Be Mindful of Caps Lock:** SHOUTING IN EMAILS IS NEVER A GOOD LOOK.
- **Avoid Jargon:** While industry-specific terms may be fine, too much jargon can alienate readers.

Real-Life Tip: A senior manager once sent an email with a frustrated tone to a junior colleague. That email was forwarded (unintentionally) to the whole team, creating unnecessary tension. Always assume your emails could be shared.

5. The Importance of a Proper Closing

End your emails on a polite and professional note. Include your contact details in your signature if the recipient may need to follow up.

- **Examples of Professional Closings:**
    - "Best regards,"
    - "Thank you,"
    - "Sincerely,"
    - For colleagues you know well: "Warm regards," or "Cheers."

Managing Your Inbox: A Key to Professional Communication

In today's workplace, your email inbox is not just a communication tool—it's a reflection of your organizational skills and responsiveness. An inbox that's cluttered or neglected can send the wrong message, while one that's well-maintained can enhance your efficiency and reputation.

The Importance of Timely Responses

Emails are often the lifeblood of professional communication, and timely responses demonstrate respect and reliability. Ignoring or delaying a reply can create bottlenecks, frustrate colleagues, and harm your credibility. Aim to respond to important emails within 24 hours, even if it's just to acknowledge receipt and promise a detailed reply later.

Pro Tip: Use templates for common responses to save time while maintaining professionalism. For example:

"Thank you for your email. I'll review the details and get back to you by [specific day/time]."

Inbox Organization Made Simple

Managing a steady stream of emails doesn't have to be overwhelming. With a few strategic habits, you can stay on top of your inbox:

- **Adopt the Two-Minute Rule**: If an email requires less than two minutes to address, handle it immediately.
- **Categorize and Prioritize**: Use folders or labels to sort emails by urgency or topic. Mark important messages for follow-up.
- **Schedule Inbox Time**: Allocate specific times in your day to check and process emails, rather than constantly monitoring your inbox.

Real-Life Example: Amal, a project manager, reduced her email backlog by dedicating the first 30 minutes of her workday to inbox management. She started prioritizing urgent requests and archiving informational emails, which helped her focus on high-value tasks.

Following Through: Beyond the Reply

Replying to emails is only part of the equation. Actioning what's requested in the email completes the communication loop. For example, if a colleague asks for a report, promptly sharing it solidifies your dependability.

By keeping your inbox organized, responding promptly, and acting on emails, you ensure that your digital communication is as polished and professional as your in-person interactions.

Phone and Video Call Etiquette: The Human Connection

While emails are great for documentation, calls—both phone and video—are essential for real-time discussions. Yet, they come with their challenges, from poor sound quality to distractions in the background. Let's explore how to handle calls with professionalism.

1. Preparing for the Call

- **Know the Agenda:** Whether it's a one-on-one or a group call, know why the meeting is happening.
- **Test Your Technology:** Check your audio and video equipment beforehand. Nothing derails a meeting like a "Can you hear me now?" loop.
- **Set Up Your Environment:** Choose a quiet location. For video calls, ensure your background is clean and non-distracting.

2. Conducting the Call

- **Speak Clearly:** Whether on the phone or video, clear enunciation is key.
- **Be Mindful of Interruptions:** Let others finish speaking before you chime in.

- **Mute When Not Speaking:** For larger calls, keep yourself muted until it's your turn to talk.

Example: During a major client call, a barking dog interrupted an otherwise professional presentation. It was a moment of levity, but it underscored the importance of choosing a quiet environment.

3. Video Call-Specific Tips

- **Dress Professionally:** Even if you're working from home, wear attire that's appropriate for the meeting.
- **Eye Contact:** Look at the camera when speaking—it simulates eye contact.
- **Engage Visually:** Nod or smile to show you're listening.

Handling Difficult Conversations

Few things in the workplace are as daunting as a difficult conversation. Whether it's giving constructive feedback, addressing a conflict, or negotiating terms, the stakes feel high. Here's how to approach these conversations with confidence.

1. Prepare Thoroughly

- **Know the Facts:** Gather all relevant information and examples before initiating the conversation.
- **Anticipate Reactions:** Think about how the other person might respond and prepare accordingly.

2. Timing is Everything

- **Choose the Right Moment:** Find a time when both you and the other person can give the conversation your full attention.

- **Avoid Rushed Discussions:** A quick chat in passing won't suffice for serious matters.

3. Approach with Empathy

Start the conversation by acknowledging the other person's perspective.

- **Example:** Instead of saying, "You missed another deadline," try, "I noticed the project timeline has been challenging. Can we talk about what's causing delays?"

4. Listen Actively

Let the other person share their side of the Example without interruption. Use phrases like, "I understand," or "That makes sense," to show you're engaged.

5. Find Solutions Together

Frame the conversation around solutions rather than blame. Use collaborative language like, "How can we address this together?"

Example: A manager once turned a tense feedback session into a brainstorming session, where the employee not only accepted the critique but also proposed their own solutions.

Bringing It All Together

Effective communication isn't just about speaking or writing—it's about encouraging understanding. By mastering email etiquette, handling calls with poise, and navigating tough conversations with empathy, you'll build stronger relationships, resolve issues more effectively, and enhance your professional reputation.

The workplace is a maze of interactions, but armed with these skills, you'll navigate it with ease. Communication isn't just a skill; it's your secret weapon for success.

3 MEETING MANNERS

Chapter 3: Meeting Manners

Meetings are a fundamental part of professional life, acting as the backbone for collaboration, problem-solving, and decision-making in the workplace. Yet, they are often met with sighs of frustration due to inefficiencies, lack of structure, or poor participation. By mastering the art of meeting manners, you can transform this often-dreaded aspect of work into an opportunity to shine, build stronger relationships, and leave a lasting impression.

In this chapter, we'll explore every aspect of meeting etiquette—from preparation and participation to follow-up and feedback—using examples, Examples, and actionable tips to help you excel.

Before the Meeting: Setting the Stage

The Power of Preparation

Preparation is not just about reviewing documents; it's about demonstrating respect for everyone's time and ensuring your contributions are meaningful. Proper preparation signals professionalism and helps you feel confident, even in high-stakes meetings.

1. **Understand the Objective**: Whether you're hosting or attending, know the purpose of the meeting. Is it a brainstorming session, a progress review, or a decision-making discussion? Clear objectives help focus your efforts.
    - *Tip*: Write down three questions or points you want to address. This keeps you engaged and ensures your contributions are aligned with the meeting's goals.
2. **Review Relevant Materials**: Skim through the agenda, previous meeting minutes, or any reports provided. Being

caught off-guard by information you should know diminishes your credibility.
    - *Example*: Imagine walking into a budget meeting and asking, "What's our current spend?" when that information was emailed in advance. Avoid this pitfall by preparing thoroughly.
3. **Anticipate Challenges**: If contentious issues are on the agenda, think about potential objections or questions others might raise. Preparing thoughtful responses will help you navigate these moments with ease.

Polishing Your Punctuality

Arriving late to a meeting sends a message: your time is more valuable than others'. Aim to be early—not just on time. This applies to virtual meetings too; a few extra minutes allow you to troubleshoot technical issues.

- **Golden Rule**: Arrive 5–10 minutes early to in-person meetings and log in 3–5 minutes early to virtual ones.
- **Example**: A colleague once walked into an important strategy meeting late, spilling coffee in the process. The distraction derailed the discussion for minutes, leaving a poor impression. Don't be that person!

Dress and Setup Matter

For in-person meetings, dress appropriately for the culture of your workplace. For virtual meetings, your background, lighting, and attire play a role in how you're perceived. A clean, professional environment demonstrates you're taking the meeting seriously.

- *Tip*: Keep your camera at eye level and test your microphone beforehand. Poor audio or visual quality can undermine your professionalism.

Hospitality Matters

If participants are traveling from another office or outside the company, arrange simple refreshments before they arrive. A pot of fresh coffee or tea, chilled water at every seat, and a small plate of light snacks (e.g., fruit or biscuits) instantly signals respect for their time and comfort. Confirm any dietary restrictions in advance, keep everything neatly arranged, and clear it away promptly when the meeting concludes. Thoughtful hospitality sets a welcoming tone and lets visitors focus on the agenda rather than their thirst or hunger.

Responding to and Attending Meetings

Meetings are the cornerstone of workplace collaboration, but how you approach them—starting from the invitation—can significantly impact your professional image. Here's how to manage meeting invites and your presence effectively.

Responding to Meeting Invites: Setting the Right Tone

1. **Acknowledge Invitations Promptly**: When you receive a meeting request, respond as soon as possible. This shows respect for the organizer's effort and helps them plan better. Even if you're unsure about your availability, reply with a tentative response and follow up once you're certain.

   Example: "Thank you for the invite. I'm checking my schedule and will confirm shortly."

2. **Clarify When Necessary**: If the agenda is unclear or if you have conflicts, don't hesitate to seek clarification or propose an alternative time. This demonstrates engagement and a proactive attitude.

Example: "Could you please share the topics we'll be discussing? I'd like to ensure I'm well-prepared."

3. **Avoid Unexplained Declines**: If you need to decline, provide a brief but polite reason and, if possible, suggest another way to contribute.

Example: "Unfortunately, I have a prior commitment during this time, but I'm happy to review the meeting notes and provide input afterward."

Attending Meetings: Make It Count

1. **Come Prepared**: Review the agenda and any pre-meeting materials in advance. Jot down key points or questions to contribute meaningfully.
2. **Be Present**: Arrive on time, whether in-person or virtually. Showing up late—or worse, multitasking—signals disinterest and disrupts the flow.
3. **Engage Thoughtfully**: Listen actively and wait for the appropriate moment to share your input. Avoid interrupting others and build on their ideas to foster collaboration.

   Example: "Building on what Fatima mentioned, I believe we can also explore…"

4. **Follow Up**: After the meeting, promptly complete any assigned tasks and thank the organizer if the session was particularly productive.

By mastering these habits, you not only show respect for your colleagues' time but also position yourself as a reliable and professional team member. Meetings, when handled well, can be opportunities to showcase your commitment and collaboration skills.

During the Meeting: Be Present, Be Polite

Listening: The Unsung Hero

Active listening is a cornerstone of meeting etiquette. It's not just about hearing words; it's about understanding and showing that you value others' contributions.

1. **Show You're Engaged**: Nod occasionally, make eye contact, and lean slightly forward to signal interest.
2. **Take Notes**: Jotting down key points helps you stay focused and demonstrates your attentiveness. Plus, it's a handy reference for follow-ups.

Speaking with Impact

When it's your turn to speak, make it count. Rambling or deviating off-topic wastes time and diminishes the value of your input.

1. **Stay Concise**: Begin with the main point and add supporting details only if necessary.
    - *Example*: Instead of saying, "I think we might want to consider looking into possibly revising the policy," try, "I suggest revising the policy to address these specific gaps."
2. **Use Inclusive Language**: Avoid jargon or acronyms that might alienate team members unfamiliar with them.
3. **Practice Empathy in Disagreements**: Disagree respectfully by focusing on ideas, not individuals.
    - *Phrase to Use*: "That's an interesting perspective. What if we also considered this angle?"

Handling Technology in Meetings

For virtual meetings, your technical etiquette is as crucial as your verbal contributions.

- **Mute When Not Speaking**: Background noise can be distracting.
- **Use the Chat Feature Wisely**: Avoid spamming with unnecessary comments. Use it for clarifications or sharing relevant links.

Encouraging Collaboration

Help foster a culture where everyone feels heard. If you're leading the meeting, actively invite quieter participants to share their views.

- *Example*: A project manager once said, "Ali, you've worked closely on this—can you share your perspective?" That small gesture encouraged team members to participate more freely.

Common Meeting Pitfalls and How to Avoid Them

1. **Meeting Overload**: If meetings are becoming excessive, propose alternatives like email updates or shorter stand-ups.
2. **Side Conversations**: Politely steer the discussion back on track: "That's an important point. Let's table it for later and focus on the current topic."
3. **Interruptions**: If you're interrupted, calmly assert yourself: "I'd like to finish my point, and then I'd love to hear your thoughts."

After the Meeting: Cementing the Outcomes

Actionable Follow-Ups

Follow-ups are where ideas become actions. Without them, meetings are just discussions.

1. **Summarize Key Points**: Whether you're the leader or a participant, take the initiative to recap the meeting's outcomes in a quick email or shared document.
    - *Tip*: Use bullet points to clearly outline action items, responsible parties, and deadlines.
2. **Deliver on Promises**: If you committed to a task, prioritize it. Consistently following through builds trust and reliability.

Seeking Feedback

Evaluate the meeting's effectiveness. For organizers, this could mean sending a quick survey to participants. For attendees, reflect on whether you contributed effectively and ask for input if needed.

Advanced Meeting Etiquette

Dealing with Hierarchies

In meetings with senior leaders, balance confidence with humility. Avoid speaking just to impress; instead, provide meaningful input.

Managing International Meetings

Global teams add complexity. Be mindful of time zones, cultural differences, and language barriers.

- *Tip*: When scheduling, rotate meeting times to accommodate all regions fairly.

Hybrid Meeting Tips

In hybrid meetings, make an extra effort to include remote participants. Address them by name to ensure they feel part of the conversation.

Why Meeting Etiquette Is a Career Game-Changer

Meetings are more than just gatherings; they're opportunities to showcase your professionalism, build relationships, and influence outcomes. By mastering meeting etiquette, you not only contribute to productive discussions but also elevate your personal brand in the workplace.

Final Thoughts

Remember, the way you handle meetings is a reflection of your respect for others' time, your ability to collaborate, and your commitment to professionalism. With preparation, thoughtful participation, and diligent follow-ups, you can turn every meeting into a career-enhancing opportunity.

4 THE SOCIAL SIDE OF WORK

Chapter 4: The Social Side of Work

Work isn't just about the job description or the tasks you complete—it's also about the relationships you build and the impressions you leave. Navigating the social aspects of work can sometimes feel like mastering a secret language, but it's a skill anyone can develop. From acing office parties to managing casual chats, your ability to handle workplace interactions can open doors to opportunities and create a more harmonious work environment.

In this chapter, we'll explore not only what to do but also what not to do, with plenty of examples, Examples, and actionable advice to help you shine in every workplace social scenario.

Office Parties and Social Events: Navigating the Fun Professionally

Office parties and social events can be fantastic opportunities to bond with colleagues, build your professional network, and even show a bit of your personality. But they're also filled with potential pitfalls. Here's how to make the most of them.

Understanding the Purpose of the Event

Before RSVPing or picking out your outfit, get a clear sense of the event's tone and purpose. Is it a formal company celebration, a team-building retreat, or a casual after-work gathering? Each requires a slightly different approach.

- **Formal Events:** For occasions like annual galas or awards ceremonies, polish your small talk and stick to professional topics. Complimenting the host or discussing the company's recent achievements are safe bets.
- **Casual Events:** For informal gatherings, it's okay to relax a bit, but remember, casual doesn't mean unprofessional.

Steer clear of controversial topics, and don't assume that relaxed rules apply across the board.

Example: At a company holiday party, Hanan noticed her CEO sitting alone and decided to strike up a conversation about the event's charitable fundraiser. That brief interaction not only made her more visible but also helped her stand out as someone engaged in the company's broader mission.

How to Dress?

Your outfit should neither be too formal nor too casual but just right for the occasion.

1. **Formal Settings:** Opt for a cocktail dress, a suit, or a combination of tailored separates in neutral tones. Accessories should be understated but elegant.
2. **Smart Casual:** This is often the trickiest category. Think neat trousers or a pencil skirt with a well-fitted blouse or button-down shirt. Avoid jeans unless they're specifically mentioned in the dress code.
3. **Casual Events:** Even at the most laid-back BBQ, avoid flip-flops, shorts, or anything that looks like it belongs at the beach.

Pro Tip: When in doubt, slightly overdress. It's easier to tone down a more formal look than to recover from looking underdressed.

Example: Jamal, a tech analyst, once attended a semi-formal company dinner in jeans and a hoodie, thinking it was casual. The result? Awkward glances and missed networking opportunities. Now, he always keeps a blazer in his car—just in case.

Making the Most of Networking Opportunities

Workplace social events are golden opportunities to meet people you might not interact with daily. But there's an art to mingling effectively.

- **Start Small:** If large groups intimidate you, begin with people you already know, then gradually expand your circle.
- **Ask Open-Ended Questions:** Instead of "Do you like working here?" try "What projects are you most excited about lately?" It's a more engaging way to connect.
- **Be Memorable, Not Loud:** Share a relevant Example or insight about work to leave a lasting impression, but avoid dominating the conversation.

Example: During an offsite event, Dana chatted with someone from another department about a recent company initiative. That brief encounter led to an unexpected cross-department collaboration and a significant boost to her career visibility.

The Dos and Don'ts of Workplace Gift-Giving

Gift-giving at work is more nuanced than it seems. Done right, it can build goodwill and promote stronger relationships. Done wrong, it can backfire or create awkwardness.

Occasions and Contexts

Gifts are usually appropriate during holidays, birthdays, retirements, or milestone achievements. However, every workplace has its culture, so observe how others handle gift-giving before diving in.

- **For Holidays:** Group gifts for managers or shared treats for the team (like chocolates or baked goods) work well.

- **For Personal Milestones:** Small, thoughtful tokens such as a book, a plant, or a gift card are ideal.

Choosing the Right Gift

The golden rule is to keep it thoughtful but professional.

- **Good Ideas:** Personalized office supplies, gourmet food items, or vouchers for experiences like coffee or lunch.
- **Avoid:** Overly personal gifts (like perfume or jewelry), gifts with hidden messages (like self-help books), or anything extravagant.

Pro Tip: Handwritten notes can elevate even the simplest gift.

Example: Mohammed once gave his retiring mentor a photo book filled with team memories. It was inexpensive but deeply meaningful, earning him kudos from colleagues and the recipient alike.

Mastering Everyday Social Interactions

The Art of Small Talk

Small talk can feel superficial, but it's often the gateway to stronger connections. The key is to show genuine interest.

- **Start Simple:** Ask about their weekend plans, hobbies, or favorite lunch spots.
- **Avoid Taboo Topics:** Politics, religion, and office gossip are conversational landmines.
- **Listen More Than You Speak:** People remember how you make them feel, not what you say.

Example: Layla, an HR manager, became known for her warm, engaging demeanor simply by asking, "What's the most interesting thing you've done this week?" during casual chats.

Navigating Gossip

Every office has its share of gossip. The trick? Stay informed without being a participant.

- If someone shares juicy news, respond neutrally: "That's interesting," and steer the conversation back to safer ground.
- Never repeat or spread unverified information. It's a surefire way to lose trust.

The Cultural Side of Socializing at Work

In a globalized workplace, cultural sensitivity is a must.

- **Learn the Basics:** In some cultures, direct eye contact signals respect; in others, it can be seen as overly assertive.
- **Food and Drink:** Be mindful of dietary restrictions and preferences at office events. Offering vegetarian or halal options, for example, shows thoughtfulness.
- **Respect for Time:** In some cultures, punctuality is paramount, while others may view schedules more flexibly.

Example: During a multinational team lunch, Talal noticed that one colleague wasn't eating due to dietary restrictions. He took note and ensured future events included more inclusive menu options, earning him respect as a considerate team player.

Exiting Gracefully

Knowing when and how to leave a social event can be just as important as how you participate.

- **Timing Matters:** For formal events, leaving after key moments (like speeches or dessert) is typically acceptable. For informal events, pay attention to cues from the host.
- **The Thank-You Exit:** Always thank the host or organizer. A simple "Thanks for putting this together" goes a long way.

Example: At a holiday party, Maryam stayed just long enough to mingle with her team and personally thank the event organizer. Her thoughtful gesture left a lasting positive impression.

Key Takeaways for Workplace Social Success

- **Be Present:** Show genuine interest in others during conversations.
- **Be Mindful:** Respect boundaries, cultural norms, and the context of each event.
- **Be Memorable:** Leave every interaction on a positive note, whether it's with a kind word or a thoughtful gesture.

By approaching the social side of work with curiosity, respect, and a dash of confidence, you'll build stronger relationships and establish yourself as someone people enjoy working with—a priceless asset in any professional setting.

Chapter 4: The Social Side of Work | 47

5 THE DIGITAL WORKPLACE

Chapter 5: The Digital Workplace

The digital age has revolutionized how we work, communicate, and collaborate. From video calls to instant messaging, social media networking, and even AI-assisted workflows, the digital workplace is a dynamic environment that demands not only technical proficiency but also the ability to navigate these spaces with professionalism and respect.

1. Social Media: Balancing Professionalism and Personality

Social media is like a window into your professional and personal life. It can be a powerful platform to showcase your expertise or a potential minefield if mishandled.

Professional Presence:

Consider Noor, a mid-level manager who used LinkedIn to share insights from a leadership workshop. Her thoughtful posts gained traction, connecting her with other industry leaders and opening doors for speaking engagements. Contrast this with Ali, whose frequent political rants on Twitter alienated colleagues and cost him a promotion when a senior leader questioned his judgment.

Platform-Specific Strategies:

- **LinkedIn:** Focus on professional achievements, industry articles, and career updates. Highlight certifications, volunteer work, or participation in conferences.
- **Facebook & Instagram:** If used personally, tighten privacy settings. For work purposes, use these platforms sparingly and thoughtfully to avoid oversharing.
- **Twitter:** Share concise professional updates or industry news. Use discretion with humor or controversial opinions.

Actionable Tips:

1. Regularly audit your online profiles to ensure they align with your desired professional image.
2. Share content that reflects your values, expertise, and interests in a positive light.
3. When in doubt, keep it private.

2. Privacy and Boundaries: Guardrails in the Digital Age

The blurring lines between work and home can make it challenging to maintain healthy boundaries.

Setting Boundaries:

Imagine Rashid, a remote worker who answered emails late into the night. While his intentions were good, his manager and team began expecting 24/7 availability, leading to burnout. By using scheduled email tools and setting clear work hours, Rashid regained balance and reduced stress.

Balancing Availability:

The rise of instant messaging tools like WhatsApp and Microsoft Teams has amplified connectivity. While helpful for quick interactions, they can promote an "always-on" culture. Be intentional about signaling your availability through status updates like "Available," "In Focus Mode," or "Out of Office."

Actionable Tips:

1. Use tools like "Do Not Disturb" or scheduled messages to control interruptions.
2. Communicate your availability to colleagues, particularly in cross-time-zone teams.

3. Avoid sending non-urgent communications outside of work hours.

3. Email and Messaging: Elevating Communication

Digital communication is both a science and an art, requiring clarity, conciseness, and professionalism.

Email Mastery:

A polished email speaks volumes. Consider Khalid, who consistently wrote well-structured emails with clear subject lines like "Budget Review: Updates Needed by Friday." His clarity impressed stakeholders and positioned him as a reliable communicator.

Conversely, vague or overly casual emails—such as "Hey, about the meeting..."—can create confusion or project a lack of seriousness.

Instant Messaging Etiquette:

Messaging apps have their own unspoken rules. Quick updates like, "Can we touch base about the quarterly updates?" are appropriate, but detailed conversations should move to email or meetings. Avoid overusing emojis or sending a barrage of messages.

Actionable Tips:

1. Use bullet points or numbered lists in emails for easier readability.
2. Limit emojis to casual chats; keep formal communication professional.
3. Follow up only after allowing a reasonable response time.

4. Video Conferencing: Your Virtual Stage

Video meetings have become the default for collaboration, but they require preparation and mindfulness to maintain professionalism.

Example: The Pajama Blunder

Sameera joined a video call wearing a blazer over her pajama top. When she stood up to adjust her chair, her mismatched attire became visible, earning chuckles but also undermining her credibility. Always dress fully, even if you think only your top half will be visible.

Best Practices:

1. **Environment:** Choose a clean, uncluttered background. If unavailable, use a neutral virtual background.
2. **Engagement:** Look directly into the camera to simulate eye contact. Smile and nod to show attentiveness.
3. **Timing:** Respect others' time by arriving early and wrapping up discussions within the allotted period.

Actionable Tips:

1. Test your audio, video, and internet connection before the meeting.
2. Use "Mute" when not speaking to avoid background noise disruptions.
3. Send follow-up summaries after the meeting to reinforce key points.

5. Digital Collaboration: Building Virtual Teamwork

The digital workplace thrives on collaboration tools like Microsoft Teams, Google Workspace, and project management platforms like Trello or Asana.

Scenario: A Communication Breakdown

In a global team, Maryam noticed delays in project delivery. Upon review, she realized miscommunication in their shared document comments had caused confusion. By implementing weekly check-ins and a shared action tracker, the team improved clarity and accountability.

Tools and Tips:

1. Use shared calendars to schedule meetings that suit all time zones.
2. Create clear naming conventions for shared files to avoid duplicates.
3. Assign responsibilities within collaboration tools to ensure accountability.

6. Cybersecurity: Protecting Your Digital Footprint

Digital interactions bring risks. Phishing scams, data breaches, and weak passwords can wreak havoc on organizations.

Example: The Costly Click

An employee unknowingly clicked a phishing link, compromising sensitive company data. This incident led to financial loss and mandatory cybersecurity training for the entire team.

Actionable Tips:

1. Use multi-factor authentication for all work accounts.
2. Avoid public Wi-Fi or use a secure VPN when accessing work systems remotely.
3. Think twice before clicking on unsolicited emails or attachments.

7. Productivity in the Digital Era

Digital tools can enhance efficiency, but without discipline, they can become distractions.

The Overloaded Inbox:

Roaya felt overwhelmed by hundreds of daily emails until she implemented a triage system: respond immediately to urgent emails, delegate tasks, and archive informational messages.

Actionable Tips:

1. Dedicate specific times to check emails and messages.
2. Use productivity apps to prioritize tasks.
3. Set boundaries for non-urgent tasks to maintain focus.

8. The Future of Digital Workplaces

The workplace continues to evolve. Staying ahead of trends will position you as a forward-thinking professional.

Emerging Technologies:

- **AI in Workflow:** Tools like ChatGPT or Grammarly enhance writing, while Trello automates task management. Embrace these tools to improve efficiency.

- **Remote Work Norms:** With hybrid models, etiquette must adapt to balance in-office and remote dynamics.

Cyber Wellness:

Encourage practices like digital detoxes to combat screen fatigue and promote mental health.

By embracing these principles, you'll not only thrive in the digital workplace but also set an example for others. Mastering digital etiquette is an ongoing journey that requires attentiveness, adaptability, and a commitment to professionalism. Let these insights empower you to navigate the complexities of the modern work environment with ease and confidence.

6 THE MULTICULTURAL WORKPLACE

Chapter 6: The Multicultural Workplace

The Value of Multiculturalism at Work

A multicultural workplace is like a vibrant tapestry woven from different threads—each culture contributes its unique patterns, colors, and textures. It brings innovation and creativity to the forefront, offering a range of perspectives that challenge the status quo. However, for this diversity to be an asset, we must invest time and effort into understanding, respecting, and celebrating cultural differences.

Think of a multicultural team as an orchestra. Each instrument has its unique sound, and when they play together in harmony, the result is breathtaking. However, without understanding the music's rhythm and flow, the performance can easily turn into a noise. Similarly, workplaces flourish when cultural diversity is embraced with sensitivity and open-mindedness.

The Foundations: Cultural Awareness and Empathy

Know Before You Go

Before you step into a culturally diverse workplace or engage with international colleagues, make it a point to learn about their cultures. Start small: What are their communication preferences? What topics are considered taboo? For example, in many Middle Eastern cultures, saying "no" directly can be seen as impolite, so a vague "we'll see" might actually mean "no." Misinterpreting these subtleties can lead to misaligned expectations.

Example: A project manager shared how a deal with a Japanese client almost fell through because the team misread their polite hesitations as agreement. After consulting a cultural expert, they rephrased their requests more diplomatically, salvaging the project and gaining a deeper understanding of Japanese business etiquette.

Action Tip: If you're working with a new culture, spend 15 minutes researching their business norms. Websites, YouTube videos, or even quick chats with experienced colleagues can provide invaluable insights.

The Golden Rule 2.0

While the original Golden Rule says, "Treat others the way you want to be treated," the multicultural version is, "Treat others the way *they* want to be treated." This requires stepping out of your own cultural lens and seeing the world from someone else's perspective.

Practical Example: An American manager might view casual first-name use as friendly, but their German counterpart might interpret it as disrespectful in a formal business setting. The solution? Start formal and adjust based on their preferences.

Bridging Cultural Communication Gaps

Verbal and Non-Verbal Communication

Words matter, but in multicultural workplaces, body language and tone can speak louder than words. For instance, a thumbs-up is a positive gesture in many countries but can be offensive in other regions. Similarly, prolonged eye contact might signal confidence in the U.S. but could be seen as confrontational in some Asian cultures.

Example: A colleague recounted how their client misunderstood crossed arms during a presentation as disinterest. After learning that this posture can be seen as closed-off in some cultures, they consciously adopted open body language, leading to a more successful interaction.

Action Tip: Use inclusive body language—open palms, nodding to show understanding, and maintaining a neutral but attentive posture.

Adapting Your Message

High-context cultures (e.g., Japan, India) rely heavily on implicit communication, reading between the lines, and understanding context. Low-context cultures (e.g., the U.S., Germany) prefer direct, explicit communication. Misalignments can cause confusion or even offense.

Example: When a Japanese colleague says, "That might be difficult," it likely means, "No, that's impossible." Similarly, when an American says, "Let's circle back," they mean, "This isn't a priority right now." Understanding these nuances can prevent unnecessary friction.

Action Tip: Confirm your understanding after discussions: "Just to clarify, are we saying this can't proceed due to resource constraints?"

Collaboration Across Cultures

Handling Conflicts: A Cultural Lens

Disputes are inevitable in any workplace, but how they are handled varies greatly across cultures. In some Middle Eastern cultures, conflict resolution might prioritize saving face, so direct confrontation is avoided. Meanwhile, in Western cultures, addressing issues head-on is often seen as constructive.

Example: A multicultural team faced tension when a U.S. member openly criticized a proposal in front of everyone, leaving their Japanese counterpart visibly uncomfortable. The manager mediated by suggesting feedback be shared privately in future meetings.

Action Tip: When addressing conflicts, ask yourself, "Is this the right forum? Would a one-on-one conversation be more appropriate?"

Time Zones and Flexibility

Remote teams spanning continents often struggle with time zones. For instance, scheduling a call between Bahrain and California means someone has to compromise on working hours. Acknowledge this and rotate meeting times to distribute the inconvenience fairly.

Action Tip: Use scheduling tools like World Clock Meeting Planner and always express gratitude when colleagues adjust their schedules to accommodate you.

Everyday Cultural Sensitivities

The Food Factor

Food is a universal connector but can also be a source of discomfort if not handled sensitively. Dietary restrictions due to religion, culture, or health should be respected. For instance, serving alcohol at a team dinner without considering Muslim colleagues could cause embarrassment and alienation.

Action Tip: When organizing meals, ask for dietary preferences beforehand. Offering a variety of options ensures everyone feels included.

Celebrating Together

Encourage employees to share their cultural traditions. Hosting events like Diwali celebrations, Chinese New Year parties, or Bahraini Ghabga gatherings during Ramadan can promote understanding and friendship.

Example: A multinational firm introduced "Culture Days," where employees could showcase food, music, and traditions from their countries. This initiative not only improved team morale but also led to unexpected collaborations as employees bonded over shared interests.

Leadership in a Multicultural Setting

Setting the Tone

As a leader, your behavior sets the standard. Make cultural sensitivity a visible priority. For instance, when onboarding international hires, include a cultural orientation session to bridge potential gaps.

Practical Example: A manager implemented "cultural buddy pairs," matching new employees with colleagues familiar with the local culture. This helped ease transitions and strengthened team bonds.

Inclusive Decision-Making

In some cultures, decisions are hierarchical, with leaders expected to take charge. In others, like Scandinavian countries, consensus is king. Balancing these approaches requires clear communication and adaptability.

Action Tip: Start meetings by outlining how decisions will be made: "For this discussion, I'd like everyone's input before I make a final call."

Personal Growth Through Cultural Competence

Curiosity Is Key

Approach cultural differences with curiosity rather than judgment. If a colleague's behavior puzzles you, ask questions respectfully. For instance, "I noticed that meetings often start later in your department—is there a specific reason for this?"

Learning by Doing

The best way to understand another culture is to immerse yourself in it. Attend cultural festivals, try new cuisines, or read books about different countries. Not only will this broaden your worldview, but it will also enhance your professional relationships.

Final Thoughts

A multicultural workplace is both a challenge and an opportunity. By cultivating cultural intelligence, you become more than just a team player—you become a bridge-builder, connecting ideas, people, and perspectives. With each interaction, you enrich your understanding and contribute to a more inclusive, harmonious, and dynamic workplace.

7 EVERYDAY ETIQUETTE

Chapter 7: Everyday Etiquette

Workplaces are bustling microcosms where relationships are built, tasks are tackled, and opportunities arise—all on a foundation of everyday etiquette. While grand gestures and standout achievements often get the spotlight, it's the small, daily habits that truly define your professional reputation. This chapter takes a deep dive into the nuances of workplace conduct, providing tips, relatable examples, and actionable advice to ensure your daily interactions contribute to a positive, respectful, and harmonious environment.

The Office Kitchen: Where Courtesy Meets Community

The office kitchen is often a litmus test for workplace civility. It's a shared space, and how you treat it reflects your respect for colleagues.

- **Cleanliness Is a Community Responsibility**

    Imagine walking into the kitchen for your morning coffee only to find a battlefield of crumbs, spills, and unwashed mugs. Frustrating, right? To keep the kitchen a stress-free zone:

    - Always clean up after yourself. If you spill coffee, grab a cloth and wipe it up.
    - Scrub your dishes or place them in the dishwasher if one is available.
    - If you microwave your lunch, cover it to avoid splatters, and wipe it clean after use.

    Tip: If you notice recurring messes, suggest a kitchen duty rota or a friendly "kitchen courtesy" poster that humorously reminds everyone to clean up.

- **The Refrigerator: A Shared Oasis**

    Office refrigerators can become a war zone of unclaimed leftovers and mysterious science experiments. Respect the space:

    - Clearly label your items with your name and the date.
    - Regularly check your food and remove expired items.
    - Don't use more space than necessary—your coworkers' meals deserve room too.

    Pro Tip: Never "borrow" someone's food without permission. If you accidentally grab the wrong item, own up to it and offer to replace it. Honesty builds trust.

- **Contributing to Communal Supplies**

    If the office stocks coffee, tea, or snacks, consider chipping in occasionally. If you finish something, let the appropriate person know—or better yet, replace it yourself. Being proactive in maintaining shared resources raises goodwill.

Noise Management: Balancing Energy and Focus

An open office can be a melting pot of creativity—or a cacophony of distractions. Managing your noise levels shows respect for others' work environments.

- **Headphones Are Your Friend**

    Listening to music, a podcast, or even a webinar? Always use headphones. But keep the volume low enough that it doesn't leak out and disrupt colleagues.

- **Calls with Care**

    Need to take a call? Find a quiet spot, like a conference room or designated phone booth. If none are available, keep your voice low and brief.

    Example: When Salman realized his booming voice carried across the office during calls, he made a habit of stepping outside. His coworkers appreciated the peace, and he appreciated the privacy.

- **Collaborative Conversations**

    If you're brainstorming or discussing a project with teammates, be mindful of your volume. Consider moving the conversation to a meeting room if it lasts more than a few minutes.

Personal Space: Respecting Boundaries

Personal space can be a sensitive issue, especially in diverse workplaces where cultural norms vary.

- **The Desk as Sacred Ground**

    Your colleague's desk is their fortress. Avoid sitting on it, moving items without permission, or borrowing supplies without asking. If you must touch something, ask first—and always return it promptly.

    Example: Reem noticed her stapler often missing. Instead of stewing silently, she placed a cheerful note on it: "I'm happy to help, but please return me to Reem's desk!" The borrowing stopped immediately.

- **Physical Boundaries**

    When talking to someone, maintain at least an arm's length of distance unless the situation or cultural context suggests otherwise. Respect their comfort zone, especially in cultures where personal space is valued highly.

Everyday Interactions: The Little Things Add Up

The way you engage with colleagues daily can shape how you're perceived. These seemingly small actions have a big impact.

- **Greetings Set the Tone**

    Never underestimate the power of a cheerful "Good morning!" It acknowledges your coworkers and promotes a sense of community. Even if you're not a morning person, a smile or a polite nod works wonders.

- **Small Talk with Purpose**

    While idle chatter can sometimes feel unproductive, strategic small talk can strengthen workplace relationships. Start with simple, inclusive questions like, "How was your weekend?" or "Any fun plans coming up?" Be genuinely interested in their response.

Time Management: Respecting Schedules and Deadlines

Your punctuality and ability to manage time reflect directly on your professionalism.

- **Arriving on Time**

    Consistently arriving late, whether for work or meetings, signals disrespect for others' time. Set reminders or alarms to ensure punctuality. If you're running late, inform the relevant people promptly.

Real-Life Fix: One manager, notorious for tardiness, started scheduling her meetings 15 minutes earlier in her calendar than the actual time. It worked like a charm, and her reputation improved.

- **Honoring Deadlines**

    Missed deadlines can ripple through a project, impacting everyone involved. If you foresee an issue, communicate early and suggest a new timeline. Transparency builds trust.

Respect for Shared Resources

From printers to paperclips, shared resources are meant to benefit everyone. Treat them with care.

- **Printing Etiquette**

    Double-check before hitting "Print." Avoid printing unnecessarily, and pick up your pages promptly to avoid clutter. If a large print job is unavoidable, consider doing it during off-peak hours.

- **Office Supplies**

    Notice the last pack of pens is gone? Let the office manager know—or better yet, place an order. Leaving others stranded without basics creates unnecessary frustration.

Creating a Positive and Inclusive Environment

Your behavior can significantly shape the workplace atmosphere.

- **Recognize and Celebrate**

    If a colleague does excellent work, acknowledge it. Simple phrases like "Great presentation!" or "Thanks for stepping up" go a long way.

- **Be Culturally Aware**

    Workplaces today are diverse. Understand and respect cultural practices, dietary restrictions, and holidays. For example, avoid scheduling team lunches during fasting periods like Ramadan.

Real-World Examples and Practical Insights

- **The Kitchen Hero**

    When her office kitchen kept running out of coffee, Zainab started a "coffee fund jar." Contributions poured in, ensuring everyone's caffeine needs were met—and Zainab became the unofficial office MVP.

- **Noise Nightmare Resolved**

    After receiving complaints about his loud typing, Ebrahim switched to a quieter keyboard. His small change improved the overall atmosphere without sacrificing productivity.

By practicing these habits daily, you'll not only earn the respect of your colleagues but also contribute to a workplace that's efficient, inclusive, and enjoyable for everyone. Remember, it's the small things—done consistently and thoughtfully—that truly define workplace etiquette.

8 LEADERSHIP AND ETIQUETTE

Chapter 8: Leadership and Etiquette

Leadership is more than a job title or set of responsibilities—it's about influence, integrity, and the ability to set an example that inspires others. Etiquette, while often seen as a "soft skill," is the backbone of effective leadership. It bridges gaps, raises trust, and creates a respectful workplace culture. This chapter explores how good manners, clear communication, and an understanding of human dynamics can elevate your leadership style and leave a lasting impact.

Leading by Example: The Cornerstone of Leadership

"Your actions speak so loudly, I can't hear what you're saying." This quote perfectly encapsulates the power of leading by example. Leaders set the tone for what's acceptable in the workplace. Whether you realize it or not, your team watches and mirrors your behavior.

What Leading by Example Looks Like

1. **Practicing Accountability:** Let's say a leader misses a deadline for a report. Instead of shifting blame, they admit, "I underestimated the time needed for this task. I'll ensure it doesn't happen again." This humility teaches the team that accountability is a strength, not a weakness.
2. **Consistency Matters:** Imagine working for someone who preaches punctuality but is always late to meetings. The inconsistency erodes respect. On the other hand, leaders who consistently adhere to their principles—whether it's about punctuality, fairness, or openness—command loyalty and admiration.
3. **Creating Psychological Safety:** As a leader, admitting you don't know everything can be powerful. Consider sharing, "I'm not familiar with this tool. Could someone walk me

through it?" Vulnerability builds trust and empowers team members to share their own uncertainties.

Building Trust Through Etiquette

Leadership thrives on trust, and good manners are one of the easiest ways to build and maintain that trust.

The Role of Small Courtesies

- **Greeting Everyone:** A simple "Good morning" as you pass through the office can humanize you in the eyes of your team. Don't underestimate the power of being approachable.
- **Thank You Goes a Long Way:** Let's say your team works late to complete a project. A leader who stops by desks to say, "Thank you for your hard work; it made a difference," leaves a lasting impression.

Listening as an Act of Respect

Listening is often overlooked but is a cornerstone of leadership etiquette.

- **Active Listening:** When a team member shares an idea, show you're engaged by maintaining eye contact, nodding, and responding thoughtfully. For example, "That's an interesting point. Can you elaborate on how it might work in our timeline?"
- **Avoiding Distractions:** Nothing undermines trust faster than checking your phone during a one-on-one conversation. Give your undivided attention—it speaks volumes.

Handling Power Dynamics with Empathy

Power can create barriers if not managed wisely. Leaders who wield power with empathy build bridges instead of walls.

Respect Across Hierarchies

A great leader values every role, from interns to executives.

- **Example:** A senior manager noticed that the janitorial staff often worked overtime but rarely interacted with the rest of the team. He organized a "Thank You Breakfast" for support staff, creating a sense of belonging across levels.

Giving Constructive Feedback

Instead of saying, "You didn't do this right," consider, "I noticed this approach didn't yield the desired results. Let's explore what might work better next time." This turns criticism into a growth opportunity.

Encouraging Collaboration

True leadership shines when a leader says, "This is a great idea. Let's refine it as a team." Inclusivity empowers employees to contribute meaningfully.

Navigating Challenging Conversations with Grace

Difficult conversations are inevitable, but good etiquette can soften their impact.

Approaching Sensitive Topics

1. **Prepare Thoroughly:** Before delivering bad news, such as a project cut or performance concerns, gather facts. This ensures you're approaching the conversation objectively.
2. **Use Empathy:** Frame discussions in a way that acknowledges the other person's feelings. For instance, "I understand this feedback may be hard to hear, but I believe it's necessary for your growth."

Resolving Conflicts

Conflict is natural, but it's the leader's job to ensure it doesn't spiral.

- **Example:** Two team members are clashing over responsibilities. A good leader says, "Let's sit down together and clarify roles so we can avoid future misunderstandings." Mediation, combined with clear communication, diffuses tension.

Promoting a Culture of Respect

Creating a culture of respect requires consistent effort and intentionality.

Actions That Promote Respect

1. **Recognize Achievements:** Publicly celebrating milestones, like completing a challenging project, builds morale. For example, "Let's all give a hand to Maryam for her innovative solution to the client's issue. It saved us time and impressed the client."
2. **Enforce Fairness:** Leaders must address bias or favoritism head-on. A good response might be, "I've noticed that

some tasks aren't distributed evenly. Let's discuss how we can balance workloads more fairly."

Global and Virtual Leadership: Expanding Etiquette's Reach

Cultural Intelligence

Working with global teams demands awareness of cultural nuances.

- **Example:** While working with a Middle Eastern team, a U.S. manager learned that scheduling meetings around prayer times earned respect and cooperation.

Virtual Team Building

- **Keep It Inclusive:** Rotate meeting times to accommodate global teams. If half your team is in the Middle East and the other in Europe, alternating times shows fairness.
- **Maintain Visibility:** In remote settings, check in regularly. A quick message like, "How's your workload this week?" can prevent employees from feeling isolated.

Recognition and Empowerment: The Ultimate Leadership Tools

Recognizing contributions and empowering your team are essential etiquette practices.

The Ripple Effect of Recognition

1. **Example:** A CEO sends handwritten thank-you notes to employees during the holiday season. It's personal, memorable, and shows genuine appreciation.
2. **Everyday Empowerment:** Instead of dictating, ask, "What do you think we should prioritize in this project?" This gives employees ownership and confidence.

Commitment to Growth and Learning

Leadership etiquette isn't static—it evolves with time and feedback.

Seeking Feedback

A simple question like, "What can I do differently to support you better?" can uncover blind spots in your leadership approach.

Lifelong Learning

Stay curious. Attend leadership workshops, read about emotional intelligence, or join peer groups to refine your skills continuously.

Conclusion: The Etiquette-Driven Leader

True leadership is about more than just results—it's about leaving a legacy of respect, empowerment, and professionalism. By integrating etiquette into your daily actions, you adopt a workplace culture where everyone feels valued. Whether it's a thoughtful "thank you," a firm handshake, or a willingness to listen, small gestures define great leaders.

Remember, leadership etiquette isn't just a skill; it's a mindset. It's about treating others the way you'd want to be treated while inspiring them to be their best. When you lead with etiquette, you not only elevate your team but also set a standard for others to follow. Let this be the foundation of your lasting impact as a leader.

9 EVOLVING ETIQUETTE

Chapter 9: Evolving Etiquette

Workplace etiquette has always been about more than just following a set of rules. It's a reflection of our adaptability, respect for others, and understanding of the social fabric that binds a professional environment together. In today's fast-paced world, where technology evolves daily and societal norms shift regularly, workplace etiquette has become a dynamic and ever-changing concept.

Adapting to Changing Norms and Expectations

Flexibility is the New Standard

The rigid office schedules of the past are increasingly giving way to flexible work arrangements. Remote work, hybrid schedules, and unconventional hours are reshaping how we think about professionalism. While these changes offer freedom, they also come with unique challenges for maintaining workplace etiquette.

For instance, in a remote environment, punctuality isn't just about showing up on time for meetings—it's about being mentally present. Logging in at the last second, unprepared, or distracted by your surroundings communicates disinterest.

Actionable Advice:

- **Maintain a schedule:** Even if you're working remotely, start and end your day at consistent times. This not only helps you stay disciplined but also makes collaboration smoother for colleagues who need to reach you.
- **Dress for success:** While working from home allows for more casual attire, dressing appropriately for video calls shows respect for your peers. A polished appearance can shift your mindset and boost your confidence.

Example: During a virtual brainstorming session, one employee stood out by showing up early, dressed professionally, and prepared with a summary of ideas. Contrast that with a colleague who joined late, camera off, and gave vague input. Guess who got asked to lead the project?

Embracing New Technologies

Every year brings a slew of tools designed to make work easier—project management apps, AI assistants, and video conferencing platforms. However, adopting new technology requires etiquette adjustments. Have you ever been in a meeting derailed by someone who didn't know how to mute their microphone? Or received an email peppered with auto-generated phrases that felt impersonal?

Tips for Navigating Tech Tools:

1. **Master the Basics:** Take time to learn the features of tools like MS Teams, Zoom, Slack, or Trello. A little preparation goes a long way in preventing embarrassing mishaps.
2. **Avoid Overuse:** Just because you can send a message at midnight doesn't mean you should. Be mindful of others' work-life balance.
3. **Use AI Thoughtfully:** Tools like ChatGPT can help draft emails or reports, but always add a personal touch to avoid sounding robotic.

Example: A manager once used a scheduling bot to plan meetings. While efficient, it repeatedly scheduled calls during employees' lunch hours, leading to frustration. A simple adjustment to block common break times solved the issue and demonstrated empathy.

Inclusive Dress Codes

As workplaces grow more diverse, so do interpretations of appropriate attire. Where a Western business suit once dominated boardrooms globally, today's dress codes are becoming more inclusive of cultural and personal expression.

Example: A young professional at a multinational firm in the Middle East shared how wearing traditional attire, like an abaya, initially felt out of place in a Westernized office culture. Over time, the company embraced cultural dress as a form of identity, making her feel respected and valued.

Pro Tips:

- When in doubt, start with business casual and adapt based on your workplace culture.
- Celebrate cultural attire by participating in "diversity days" or special occasions where colleagues share their heritage.
- Keep a backup blazer or formal outfit handy for unexpected high-level meetings.

Future Trends in Workplace Etiquette

Respect for Diversity and Inclusion

Inclusion isn't just a buzzword; it's becoming a cornerstone of workplace culture. This means being aware of microaggressions, unconscious biases, and language that can alienate colleagues.

Actionable Advice:

- Use inclusive language. For example, say "team members" instead of "guys".

- Avoid assumptions. Not everyone celebrates the same holidays. Tailor events to be inclusive, offering different options or flexible participation.
- Participate in unconscious bias training to increase cultural awareness.

Example: A company organized a team-building retreat that coincided with Ramadan. By offering alternative meal options and adjusting schedules for prayer times, they showed consideration and earned the trust of their Muslim employees.

The Mental Health Revolution

The stigma around mental health is fading, but this progress demands its own etiquette. While it's important to normalize conversations, respecting privacy and boundaries is equally critical.

How to Show Support:

- Create a culture where employees feel comfortable asking for mental health days without fear of judgment.
- Listen actively if someone opens up about stress but don't pressure them to share more than they're comfortable with.
- Encourage managers to lead by example, openly discussing stress management strategies or counseling resources.

Sustainability as a Workplace Norm

Sustainability isn't just a corporate goal—it's becoming a personal responsibility for employees.

Practical Steps to Show Environmental Etiquette:

- Bring your own reusable coffee mug or water bottle to the office.
- Use digital note-taking apps instead of printing meeting agendas.
- Turn off your monitor and unplug chargers at the end of the day.

Professionalism in a Casual Environment

As offices adopt open layouts, casual dress codes, and even game rooms, the line between work and leisure blurs. Navigating this space requires skill.

Golden Rules for Casual Settings:

- Stay professional, even during informal chats. A joke about the boss might be funny at the moment but could harm your reputation later.
- Respect boundaries. Just because your coworker shares a meme doesn't mean they want to connect on Instagram.

Respecting Modern Work Relationships

Remote and Hybrid Teams

Working remotely doesn't mean relationships should become distant. Small gestures, like starting meetings with a quick check-in about everyone's weekend, can go a long way.

Example: A manager of a hybrid team sent care packages to remote employees to make them feel as connected as their in-office counterparts.

Continuous Learning and Adaptation

The hallmark of a professional in today's world is adaptability. Whether it's learning a new tool, understanding generational differences, or embracing new cultural norms, the willingness to evolve is key.

Takeaways for Lifelong Growth:

- Regularly seek feedback, not just from peers but also subordinates.
- Attend seminars, webinars, and training sessions to stay updated on workplace trends.
- Reflect on your own biases and habits that might need changing.

Example: A senior executive who once resisted using social media realized its potential after attending a LinkedIn workshop. He not only built a strong professional network but also shared leadership insights that inspired his team.

By staying curious, empathetic, and open to change, you'll not only adapt to the evolving workplace but thrive in it. Evolving etiquette isn't just about rules; it's about relationships, respect, and readiness for what's next.

CONCLUSION: ELEVATING YOUR CAREER THROUGH THE POWER OF ETIQUETTE

Conclusion: Elevating Your Career Through the Power of Etiquette

As we come to the end of this journey through workplace etiquette, it's essential to reflect not just on what we've learned, but on why it all matters. Etiquette isn't a set of stiff, old-fashioned rules. It's the art of building trust, showing respect, and creating connections. Think of it as the foundation of a successful career and a harmonious workplace. It's the little things we often overlook that, collectively, have the power to transform how others perceive and respond to us.

Why Workplace Etiquette Is More Than Politeness

Etiquette, at its core, is about mindfulness. It's about thinking beyond yourself and considering how your actions impact those around you. Imagine a workplace where everyone showed up on time, greeted each other warmly, handled conflicts with grace, and communicated with clarity and empathy. What would that feel like? Easier? Happier? More productive? That's the magic of good manners—they're like oil in the machinery of professional life, making everything run smoother.

Take Maryam, for example, who worked in a fast-paced marketing agency. She was talented but often skipped small courtesies, like replying to emails promptly or thanking her colleagues for their help. Over time, people began to view her as inconsiderate, which impacted her ability to build strong professional relationships. Realizing this, she made an effort to change—sending quick thank-you notes, listening more in meetings, and showing appreciation for her team. The result? A noticeable improvement in collaboration and her standing in the company.

Now compare that to Ebrahim, a junior analyst who, despite being new to his firm, consistently practiced good etiquette. He was always prepared for meetings, showed respect to everyone from the receptionist to the CEO, and was quick to offer help when needed. His professionalism stood out, and within a year, he was entrusted with higher-level responsibilities.

The difference between Maryam's early struggles and Ebrahim's rapid success wasn't about their skills or intellect—it was about their approach to the people around them. Etiquette might seem like a small thing, but its impact is profound.

Summing Up the Benefits of Etiquette

Let's revisit some key themes we've explored throughout this book, with added depth and practical examples to drive home their importance:

1. **First Impressions Are Everything:** Picture walking into a room for an important meeting. You're dressed appropriately, offer a firm handshake, and greet everyone with a warm smile. These simple actions send a message: "I'm confident, prepared, and respectful." First impressions may only take seconds to form, but they linger long after the moment has passed. Think about small tweaks like keeping your LinkedIn profile picture polished or learning how to introduce yourself concisely in networking events—these are modern extensions of traditional etiquette.
2. **Communication Makes or Breaks Relationships:** Ever received a cryptic or abrupt email that left you unsure how to respond? Now imagine receiving an email that's clear, polite, and sets the right tone. Which sender would you prefer to work with? The way you write emails, conduct video calls, or even handle instant messaging speaks volumes about your professionalism. A good rule of thumb? Treat every form of communication as if it were face-to-face. Whether it's adding a cheerful greeting in your emails or pausing to listen carefully during meetings, these small habits build rapport and trust.

3. **The Power of Inclusivity:** A multicultural workplace isn't just about diversity—it's about creating an environment where everyone feels respected and valued. Simple gestures, like learning to pronounce a colleague's name correctly or avoiding assumptions about their cultural norms, show that you care. Ahmed, a team leader, once introduced an "International Food Thursday" in his office, encouraging everyone to share a dish from their culture. This small initiative broke down barriers and brought the team closer together.
4. **Digital Etiquette for a Modern World:** The rise of remote work and digital communication has added layers of complexity to workplace etiquette. It's no longer just about how you present yourself in person but also how you appear on-screen. A cluttered Zoom background or constant interruptions can detract from your professionalism. Consider Hind, who was known for her chaotic video calls, often struggling with tech issues or speaking over others. When she started prepping five minutes in advance and muting herself unless speaking, her virtual presence became more polished and effective.
5. **Handling Social Interactions With Finesse:** Office parties, team-building events, and casual coffee chats are as much a part of work as presentations and deadlines. Yet, these social situations can be a minefield. Should you talk about work at an office lunch? How do you navigate gift-giving in professional settings? The answer lies in balance. Use these moments to build friendship without forgetting your professional boundaries. For instance, bringing a thoughtful but neutral gift for a colleague's promotion—like a plant or a book—strikes the perfect tone.
6. **Everyday Courtesies Count:** Never underestimate the power of small gestures. Holding the elevator door, saying "good morning," or cleaning up after yourself in the office kitchen might seem insignificant, but they contribute to a

culture of respect. These actions say, "I value this space and the people in it."

Actionable Steps to Keep Growing

Mastering etiquette isn't a one-and-done task. It's a journey, and here's how you can keep moving forward:

- **Seek Feedback:** Ask a trusted colleague or mentor, "How do I come across in meetings?" or "Is there anything I could do better in my communication?" Their insights might reveal blind spots and help you improve.
- **Emulate Role Models:** Identify someone in your workplace who exudes professionalism and respect. What do they do differently? Observe and adapt those habits to your own style.
- **Invest in Continuous Learning:** Books, workshops, and even casual conversations can provide new perspectives on workplace behavior. Staying curious ensures you're always evolving.
- **Lead By Example:** Whether you're a team leader or not, others will notice your behavior. By practicing good etiquette consistently, you inspire those around you to do the same.

Looking Ahead: The Future of Workplace Etiquette

The workplace of tomorrow will be shaped by trends like AI, remote work, and an increasing emphasis on mental health and inclusivity. How can you prepare? Stay adaptable. Whether it's learning the etiquette of working with AI tools or understanding how to navigate a multi-generational workforce, flexibility will be your biggest asset.

Final Thoughts: Building a Legacy of Respect

In the end, etiquette isn't just about impressing others—it's about building a professional legacy. It's about creating an environment where people feel respected, valued, and motivated to do their best. Whether you're starting out in your career or are a seasoned professional, the principles of good etiquette will serve you well.

Remember, the smallest actions—offering a kind word, sending a thoughtful thank-you note, or simply listening—can have the biggest impact. So, go forth with confidence. Make every interaction an opportunity to practice kindness, professionalism, and respect. You're not just shaping your career; you're shaping the workplace around you.

Share Your Thoughts: Leave a Review

If you found the insights and guidance in this book helpful, please consider sharing your experience by leaving a review on Amazon. Your feedback not only supports me as an author but also helps others discover the value of etiquette in professional success.

Simply scan the QR code below to visit the book's page and leave your review.

Thank you for helping to spread the word about the power of workplace etiquette!

www.ingramcontent.com/pod-product-compliance
Lightning Source LLC
Chambersburg PA
CBHW030442220526
45464CB00006B/2383